# ANDREW JACKSON

By Linda Wade

Illustrated by
James Uttel

Acknowledgement: Special thanks to Joy Dunn, Director of Education at the Hermitage, home of Andrew Jackson, located near Nashville, Tennessee.

© **1993 January Productions, Inc.** All rights reserved, including the right to reproduce the book or parts in any form.

Library of Congress Catalog Card No. 074519
Printed in the United States of America
ISBN 0-87386-090-X (Paperback Edition)
ISBN 0-87386-091-8 (Library Edition)

# ANDREW JACKSON

Andrew Jackson's parents, Andrew and Elizabeth Jackson, were farmers from Northern Ireland. They had sailed to America in 1765, bringing with them their two sons, Hugh and Robert. The family settled in the Waxhaws community on the border between North Carolina and South Carolina.

Mr. Jackson built a cozy little cabin. He cleared enough land so he could plant food for his family. Things were going well—until tragedy struck! Mr. Jackson died. Mrs. Jackson was left alone with her two little children and expecting a third at any moment. She moved into a frontier log cabin with her sister. A few days later—on March 15, 1767—little Andrew was born.

When Andrew was still an infant, his mother took him and his brothers to live with another sister, Jane Crawford. James and Jane Crawford had a big home. They also had eight children! Life was never boring!

Elizabeth Jackson had hoped her youngest son would become a minister. When he was about seven years old she sent him to the Waxhaws Presbyterian Church school. Two years later she sent him to a nearby boarding school run by William Humphries. There he studied reading, writing, grammar and geography.

Andrew was especially fascinated by his teacher's map. Many of the rivers and towns on it were new to him. But some had familiar names. War had broken out between the British and the Americans. Andrew had read about some of those places in the newspaper. Mr. Humphries helped the children locate the battle areas on the map. All of a sudden the war seemed a bit more real!

When Andrew was about twelve, his Uncle John asked him to accompany him on a three-day cattle drive to the city of Charles Town (now Charleston). Andrew was thrilled. He had the beginner's job of collecting the stray cattle and keeping them in line. Because he was behind all the cattle, the dust was thick and nearly choked him; nevertheless, he was thrilled to be taking part in the drive.

He especially enjoyed the evenings. He listened as the men talked about the big town—the cock fights, the beautiful ladies, the well-dressed gentlemen. Andrew told his brothers that one day he would be one of those gentlemen!

All too soon it was time to return to the Waxhaws. Andrew gave his wages to his mother, and she arranged for him to attend an academy a few miles away. She still wanted him to become a preacher. Although Andrew did not share in this desire, he did enjoy the school. He took part in sports and made friends easily. He also got a reputation as a tough, but fair fighter.

Meanwhile the war headed south. Robert Crawford, Andrew's uncle, raised a company to protect the border settlements of South Carolina. When the British arrived early in 1780, Andrew's brother Hugh was among those killed. Andrew helped to bury the dead. As a boy he had enjoyed playing war games. But this was real. The smell was horrible. And the wounded didn't get up and start all over! Andrew was only thirteen, but he had made up his mind what he had to do.

Andrew and his older brother Robert had decided to join the army. When they told their mother, she cried. She had just lost one son. The thought of losing her other two boys was almost too much to bear. Andrew stood tall and said, "Someone's got to lick the British!" Mrs. Jackson knew she couldn't stop them. She watched them leave the next morning.

It took the boys a few days to find their uncle's company. Soon, however, they were sworn in and assigned their duties. Before long, word reached them that British soldiers were in the area. The men took a firm stand in the Waxhaws church, but the British set the church on fire. Robert and Andrew managed to escape. They found their way to a nearby cabin.

Unfortunately, the British soldiers found the cabin and barged in. They began wrecking the room. Andrew tried to slip out, but an officer saw him.

"You there!" the officer shouted. "Clean my boots!"

Andrew stood straight and faced the man. "I may be your prisoner," he said, "but I will not clean your boots!"

The British soldiers stared. No one moved. Anger welled up inside the officer. His face, neck and ears grew red. Then he lifted his sword and swung it at Andrew.

Andrew raised his left arm to protect himself. The arm saved his life; however, the sword cut his wrist to the bone and gashed his head. Andrew staggered. Blood spurted.

"Tie him up!" the officer ordered. Then he changed his mind. "I have a better use for him," he said. "He surely knows the way to that rebel named Thompson. Make him show you the way."

Someone quickly bound Andrew's wounds before the angry officer added, "Make him run. Kill him if he misleads you!"

Andrew's head was throbbing. Hatred clouded his mind. Then he felt the soldier's musket prodding him. He knew he must run and yet think clearly. Knowing that the British wanted to kill Mr. Thompson, Andrew took the longest route possible. He hoped that Mr. Thompson would see them from across the field and flee. His plan worked. When they reached the cabin, Mr. Thompson was gone.

Then Andrew was returned to the British officer. This time he was made to walk forty miles to the prison camp in Camden, South Carolina. He was given neither food nor water. When he finally arrived, he found that many of the prisoners at the camp were dying of smallpox. His brother Robert was among the ill.

When Robert and Andrew were finally released in a prisoner exchange, Mrs. Jackson came to get them. It took several days for the three of them to reach their home. Robert was barely conscious; he soon died. Andrew had a high fever, but he slowly recovered.

As soon as Andrew was well enough to care for himself, his mother left to help nurse the prisoners at Charles Town. She had received word that her nephews were there. Sadly, she, too, became ill and died. She was buried in an unmarked grave in Charles Town. At fourteen years of age, Andrew Jackson was alone.

For a while he drifted from relative to relative. In 1783 he received an inheritance from a relative in Ireland; however, he gambled most of it away. By the next year, he seemed to settle down and become more serious. He even taught school for a short time in a Waxhaws settlement.

Andrew finally settled in Salisbury, North Carolina. In December 1784 he began to study law in an office there. On September 26, 1787, he was admitted to the bar of that state. He felt very proud the first morning he walked into court. He wore a new broadcloth coat and a ruffled shirt. His red hair was plastered smooth with bear grease. He wanted to look the part of a distinguished lawyer. And that he did!

In 1788 Andrew Jackson went to the Cumberland region. He had been appointed prosecuting attorney of the western district of North Carolina—the region soon to become the state of Tennessee. On October 26, 1788, Andrew and his two lawyer friends with whom he was travelling, reached the frontier settlement of Nashville. Nashville was the judicial seat of the district.

Jackson's main duties as public prosecutor involved the collection of debts. He was very good at his job. It didn't take long for him to develop a thriving private practice. He built up a good reputation as a fearless attorney who would help a creditor collect his debts! The Tennessee landowners and creditors whose friendship and respect he gained would later become his political allies!

While in Nashville, Andrew boarded with the widow of Colonel John Donelson. He fell in love with Mrs. Donelson's daughter Rachel. Rachel was married, but was separated from her husband. Thinking that a divorce had been granted, Andrew and Rachel were married in August 1791. Later the couple learned that the divorce had not been made final until September 1793. Andrew and Rachel were remarried in January 1794.

In 1796 Tennessee was admitted to the Union as the sixteenth state. Jackson was elected as the state's first representative in Congress, but he resigned after one year. Although he had vowed to stay out of politics, he was elected to the United States Senate and he accepted the office. After one year he resigned that office, too. He had personal financial problems that needed his attention. A few months later—in September 1798—Jackson was appointed a judge in the Superior Court of Tennessee. It was a post he would hold for six years.

In 1802 Andrew Jackson received an honor that pleased him more than any he had ever received. The officers of the Tennessee militia elected him major general. He would still hold this rank years later when the War of 1812 would begin—a war that would bring him fame and glory.

Andrew Jackson had many fine qualities: He was honest. He was courageous. He was devoted to the ideals of democracy. But he had one great fault, too: his quick temper. Because of this temper, he was involved in a duel in which he killed a man.

In 1806, a lawyer named Charles Dickinson accused Jackson of being a "worthless scoundrel...and a coward." A duel was called and it was decided that Dickinson be allowed to shoot first. Dickinson bragged that the coat button over Jackson's heart was to be his aim. Knowing that Dickinson was a perfect shot, Jackson unbuttoned his coat so that the button was no longer over his heart. When Dickinson fired, the bullet broke two ribs. Jackson, his boots filling with blood, took careful aim and killed Dickinson on the spot. Jackson was forced to remember that duel to his death, for the bullet was never removed.

By this time Andrew Jackson and his wife Rachel were living on the 425-acre farm which they had purchased in 1804. (This farm, called *The Hermitage,* reached 1,500 acres in the late 1830's and comprised 1,000 acres at the time of Jackson's death in 1845.) For seventeen years, the couple lived in the simple cabins which were on the property. Then in 1821 they moved into the mansion which they had started to build two years earlier. It was a relatively simple, two-story brick home built in the Federal style.

The farm was self-sufficient. Cotton was the main cash crop. But corn, oats, wheat, peas and other crops were grown as well. Farm animals were also important. Cows and pigs provided important food products. Sheep provided wool with which to make their cloth; the wool was also sold at the market. Fine thoroughbred horses were also raised. Of course, the maintenance of such a farm was a huge task. The Jacksons had 100 slaves to help with the work.

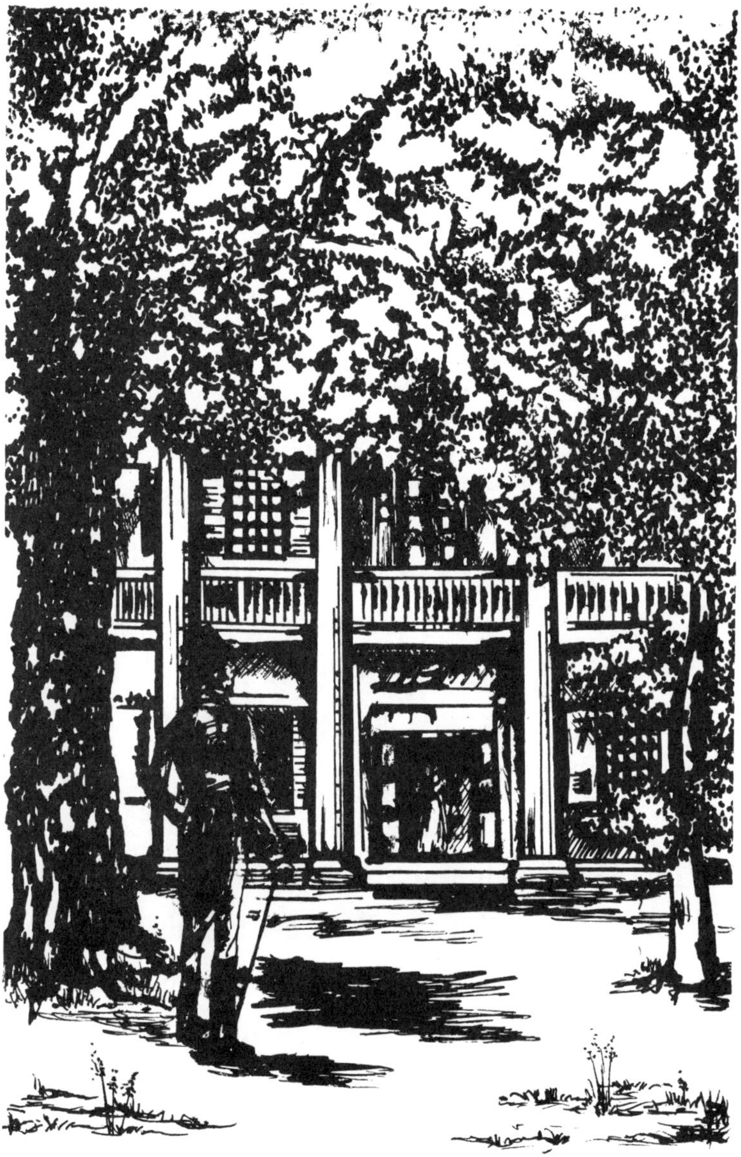

In 1812 the United States declared war against Great Britain. Since 1804 Great Britain had been seizing American ships on the open seas and searching them for British deserters. It was hard to tell the British from the Americans. They often removed American seamen and impressed them into the British navy!

Since the state of Tennessee had first given him the rank of major general ten years earlier, Jackson had been anxious to assume command of the Tennessee volunteers. He immediately offered his services to President James Madison.

His first assignment was to reinforce American troops in New Orleans. But when Jackson arrived in Natchez, Mississippi, he was told to disband. He was furious. The federal government had provided neither food, transportation, nor medicine for his men. Jackson refused to release them on their own. Instead he signed personal notes for needed food and supplies and led them home through the 500 miles of wilderness. A long time would pass until finally he would be reimbursed.

"He's tough," one soldier said of Jackson.

"Tough as hickory," came the reply from another soldier who was marching with the aid of a hickory cane. From that time on, Jackson would be nicknamed Old Hickory.

Finally, Jackson was given a command in the field. The Creek Indians, aided by the British, were threatening the southern frontier. Jackson and his men waged a campaign against the Creeks that lasted for about five months. In 1814 the Creeks were defeated and forced to surrender a large area of land to the federal government. This opened up a vast new area for settlement. It also made Jackson a hero to those western settlers.

It was after one of the battles against the Creeks—the Battle of Tallushatchee—that another side of Jackson became evident. Jackson and his men entered the Creek village. There he saw a small Indian boy lying in bed and he inquired about the child. He was told that the boy had been found at the side of his dead mother. Jackson called an aide and instructed him to take the child, called Lincoyer, to Nashville. He said that he and Mrs. Jackson would raise him as one of their family. The boy would remain with the Jacksons until his death at age 16 in 1828.

Meanwhile the war with Britain continued to rage. Andrew Jackson was sent to New Orleans, for it was certain that the city would be attacked. With the reinforcements he received, he would have about 5,000 men to defend the city.

On January 8, 1815, the British army of more than 8,000 men began its attack. It ended in terrible defeat for the British. Ironically, this had been an unnecessary battle. A peace treaty between the United States and Great Britain had been signed on December 24, 1814, at Ghent, Belgium. But news traveled slowly then.

With this great victory, Andrew Jackson returned to Nashville a national hero. Necessary or not, the defeat of the British at New Orleans made the Americans feel good about themselves.

Jackson remained in command of the army's Southern Division. In December 1817, he received vague orders to deal with the unrest along the Georgia/Florida border. The Seminole Indians, runaway slaves and outlaws from the Spanish territory of Florida had been crossing the border and raiding American settlements. Jackson boldly chased the raiders into Florida. He captured two Spanish posts and unseated the Spanish governor. Although Spain protested these actions, in the end it was forced to sell Florida to the United States. Andrew Jackson became the first American governor of Florida; however, he was unhappy there and after eleven weeks, he returned to Nashville.

Now Andrew Jackson had the time to look after his beautiful farm, The Hermitage. For their home, he ordered the furniture and draperies that Rachel had long wanted. He enjoyed receiving visitors to his farm and entertaining them in their elegant home! Andrew Jackson had become one of those dignified country gentlemen he had admired as a young man.

Although Jackson insisted that he had no interest in becoming President of the United States, people began to think of him as a possible candidate. They remembered his bravery during the War of 1812 and called him the Hero of New Orleans. Newspapers in Nashville called for his nomination. In 1822 the Tennessee legislature formally nominated him as a candidate for President. The next year it elected him to the United States Senate. It was evident that Jackson had strong support in his home state!

The political society of Washington was impressed by this country gentleman, who by now was himself showing interest in the presidency. However, John Quincy Adams, Henry Clay and William H. Crawford were also leading candidates for the 1824 election. Although Jackson received the greatest number of popular votes, a majority of the electoral votes was needed to win. None of the candidates got that majority; therefore, the election went to the House of Representatives. John Quincy Adams was elected sixth President of the United States. Jackson resigned from the Senate in 1825 and returned home.

The campaign to elect Jackson President in 1828 seemed to begin as soon as the last one ended. This time the campaign became bitter. Supporters of each candidate began to say nasty things about the other. Rachel's divorce mix-up became an issue. She had become ill, and the scandalous talk did much to worsen her condition.

Jackson defeated Adams by an electoral vote of 178 to 83. He was the first President to come from the land west of the Appalachians. He was also the first President to be elected by appealing to the mass of the voters—the common people. They could identify with him. He had a limited education and truly was a self-made man. To them, Jackson symbolized democracy.

Sadly, on December 22, 1828, Rachel Jackson died. She never got to see her husband take office. Andrew Jackson left for Washington a hurt and bitter man.

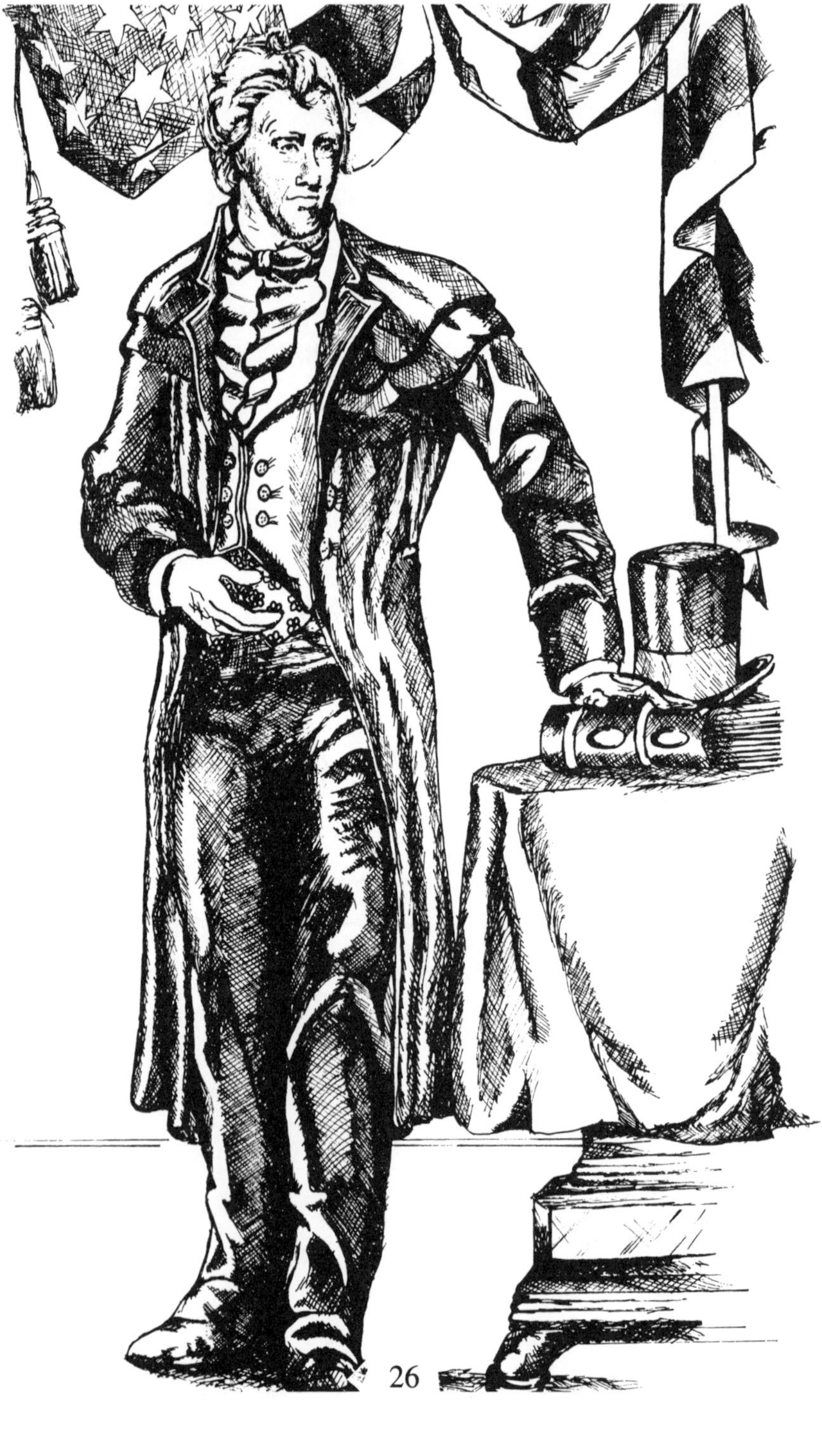

Jackson still felt that deep loss when he was sworn in as the seventh President of the United States. But the people loved this tall, blue-eyed soldier and they wanted to welcome him as President. They followed him as he rode his horse down Pennsylvania Avenue. Mob-like, they swarmed into the White House to be near him. They damaged furniture, tore draperies and broke beautiful china. They spilled cake, ice cream and punch onto the carpet. Finally, Jackson had to escape through a window.

When Jackson took office, he began to replace some of the officeholders who had supported Adams with people who had supported him. This system later became known as the "spoils system." Jackson was not the first to practice such a system. Neither did he use it as widely as his opponents sometimes charged. Actually, in his eight years as President, he replaced less than one fifth of all the federal officeholders.

A major issue of President Jackson's first administration was the tariff. The state of South Carolina blamed the tariff for its economic problems. Vice President John C. Calhoun was from that state. He said that if the people of a state believed a law passed by Congress to be unconstitutional, they could declare it null and void. The conflict between the Jackson and his vice president grew.

In 1832 a new tariff measure was passed. Although it was lower than the first, the people of South Carolina were not satisfied. That same year the legislature of South Carolina adopted the Ordinance of Nullification. It declared that the tariff acts of 1828 and 1832 were null and void. It also threatened to secede if the federal authorities tried to enforce the tariff.

President Jackson denounced the ordinance. He asked Congress to pass an act to give him authority to enforce federal laws within a state. He also asked Congress to reduce the tariff rates. Congress did both. As a result, in March 1833 South Carolina repealed its Ordinance of Nullification; in a contradictory act, however, it also declared the new Force Act to be null and void. In any case, war had been averted, and Old Hickory had gained a reputation as a strong leader!

In 1832 Jackson was nominated by the Democratic Party for a second term. Martin Van Buren was nominated as his vice president. It was the first election in which the candidates were chosen by a nominating convention. Jackson was elected President over Henry Clay by a wide margin.

Andrew Jackson was very popular. But not everyone was pleased with him. In 1830 President Jackson had signed the Indian Removal Act. It provided for the removal of Indians to lands west of the Mississippi River. Cherokee, Creek, Choctaw and Chickasaw Indians were among the hardest hit. They did not want to leave their homes and their farms. But President Jackson was not sympathetic. He ignored the treaties securing their land. He did nothing to see that Supreme Court rulings made in their favor were carried out.

Although the original bill contained no provision for force, force was eventually used. A year after President Jackson left office, about 100,000 people were made to abandon their lands. They were marched by United States troops across the country to Indian Territory, now Oklahoma. The Cherokees call their terrible trek of 1838-1839 the Trail of Tears.

President Jackson also had to deal with the issue of the Second Bank of the United States. The Bank controlled credit and currency throughout the United States. Jackson felt that it had too much authority. He also believed that the rich and powerful would use it for their own gains. The Bank's charter was due to expire in 1836. When the bill to recharter it came before him in 1832, President Jackson vetoed it. He gradually withdrew all government deposits from the Bank. The funds were re-deposited in banks all over the country. Jackson had won this battle, but hard economic times lay ahead.

In July 1836—shortly before the end of his term—President Jackson issued the Specie Circular. This ordinance required the Treasury to accept only gold or silver, which were known as specie, as payment for public land. The demand for specie became so great that many banks could not redeem their own notes. Banks began to fail. In time hundreds of banks would go out of business. But panic would not strike the nation until after President Jackson's term had ended.

Jackson gave his Farewell Address to the American people on March 4, 1837, the day of Martin Van Buren's inauguration. Jackson left office even more popular than when he had entered it.

Jackson returned to The Hermitage. For most of his remaining years, he was an invalid. But he was very proud—proud of his American heritage and proud of what he had accomplished.

Andrew Jackson died on June 8, 1845. He was 78 years old. He was buried beside Rachel in the garden of The Hermitage.